Desire for a Beginning
Dread of One Single End

Edmond Jabès

Desire for a Beginning
Dread of One Single End

translated from the French
by Rosmarie Waldrop

images
by Ed Epping

Granary Books
New York City 2001

Desire for a Beginning Dread of One Single End was first
published in France in 1991 as *Désir d'un commencement
Angoisse d'une seule fin* with images by Claude Garache.
Grateful acknowledgement is extended to Fata Morgana for
permission granted to make this edition.

First published in 2001
Printed and bound in Hong Kong

Granary Books, Inc.
307 Seventh Avenue #1401
New York, New York 10001
www.granarybooks.com

Distributed to the trade by
D.A.P. (Distributed Art Publishers)
155 Avenue of the Americas, 2nd Floor
New York, New York 10013
Orders: 1.800.338.BOOK
Tel: 212.627.1999 Fax: 212.627.9484

Library of Congress Cataloging-in-Publication Data

Jabès, Edmond
 [Désir d'un commencement. English]
 Desire for a Beginning; Dread of One Single End / Edmond
 Jabès;
translated from the French by Rosmarie Waldrop ; images
and design by Ed Epping.
    p. cm.
 ISBN 1-887123-38-5
I. Title: Desire for a beginning ; Dread of one single end. II.
Waldrop, Rosmarie. III. Epping, Ed, 1948- IV. Jabès, Edmond.
Angoisse d'une seule fin. English. V. Title: Dread of one single
end. VI. Title.
 PQ2619.A112 D4313 2001
 848' .91407–dc21
                        00-008975

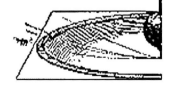

longer

$\downarrow$

$-2,\ldots$

Desire for a Beginning

" …a book – he said – that I'll never write because nobody can, it being a book:

" – against the book.

" – against thought.

" – against truth and against the word.

" – a book, then, that crumbles even while it forms.

" – against the book because the book has no content but itself, and it is nothing.

" – against thought because it is incapable of thinking its totality, let alone nothing.

" – against truth because truth is God, and God escapes thought; against truth, then, which for us remains legendary, an unknown quantity.

" – against the word, finally, because the word says only what little it can, and this little is nothing and only nothing could express it.

"And yet I know:

" – that the book is written against the book that tries to destroy it.

" – that thought thinks against the thought that covets its place.

" – that truth comes through the lived moment as the one moment to be lived.

" – that the word in vanishing reveals the very distress of man who vanishes with it. "

To take leave of the light. Propitious night. Black is the color of eternity.

As the shad roils its world of water, so memory stirs up shadows.

To make a clean draft of our ideas, having put them to soak

To think of origin, is that not first of all to test the origin?

Desire for a beginning.

(Ah this book, this book that would be mine like my heart and my eyes, like my hands and legs.

This book that fills my thought.

But if asked: "What are you thinking of? You seem preoccupied," I answer without fail:

"Of nothing."

This Nothing, my only book?)

If, as Heraclitus wrote, "Lightning creates the universe," we can perhaps say that the wound creates man.

As the stars have risen from the abyss of night so man, in the second half of the twentieth century, has been born from the ashes of Auschwitz.

Do not obstruct the course of the river.
Let dreams of water determine it.

Even when thirsty, avoid polluted water.
You will know it by its troubled transparency.
It has all the clarity of the impure.

Evidence, like the void it evicts, is disturbing, for it harries the truth it has deserted.
Shiny stars, always in conflict with their past.
Glittering nothingness.

A look, undatable.
Horizon memory.

A block of ice is nothing but a limited quantity of water surprised by the cold.
Then it has only one reason to be: to freeze something in its turn.

At death's door, it is not the future of the soul that worries us, but how the body behaves.

The soul is a bird of oblivion with many-colored wings.

What does a book show us? – First, the author's distress. Then his shamelessness.

Serpent may be a word so drawn out that it cannot help crawling along its own shadow.

Cruel humiliation.

Intolerable.

Its venom, however – Vengeance. Vengeance – reconciles it to life.

Death deprives the bird of the organs of flight essential to it.

So high must it fly into the night that its wings – the frail wings of life – are now useless, and superfluous its round, wide open eyes.

Close ties, nothing banked with nothing.

Beautiful dream expunged, O bank already flooded.

What flows with us has the role and goal to sink.
Objectivity of loss.

But each instant opposes the mind with flat denial.

One possible approach to the universe is simply to approach the possible.

Here the impossible comes up against the perennial problem of being inconceivable, a crucial problem that it keeps evading.

There will always be an impossible, undermined by possibility.

If we are warmly dressed we do not fear the cold. If we are naked we dread sunburn as much as frostbite.

To expose ourselves means accepting in advance to pay the price of our boldness.

The wholly unprotected word keeps telling us this, but we no longer listen.

Serene old age, like a blindfold.
The kindness of age.

Do not draw only on love for the strength to love. Draw also on its own royal strength.

If the world has a meaning, so has the book. But what is it?

Passive reason. Reason of the abyss.

My father – I have written this before – at the registrar's office declared me born two days before my actual birth.

Ever since, I have lived beside another self, my senior by forty-eight hours.

In the Middle Ages, in the Spain of the Inquisition, certain "repentant Jews" named "Marranos," most of whom had only accepted to convert in order to escape expulsion or the death penalty, carried in a well-hidden pocket fitted into the lining of one of their wide sleeves – usually the left – a tiny book with commentaries on the Torah or with the prayers of their childhood.

Thus, while making a show of humble submission to the implacable masters' will, they could at any time stroke with their free hand, through the dense material that protected it from being seen, the book of their ancestors and reaffirm with this secret, but O how significant, gesture their loyalty to the words of their invisible and now also silent God.

"Accept prophecies for what they are," said a sage. "They have long since stopped emitting light."

And he hurled the stone in his hand against the wall where his shadow mocked him.

This respected philosopher held that truth was half Jewish and half Christian.

Since absolute Truth is but the excessive ambition of any truth, the question we might well feel entitled to ask is this: "How can we divide in two what is always in a state of becoming?"

"Having the book as witness," wrote a sage, "is having the entire universe vouch for us."

Saved by the saved book.

The Jew faces the Jew, as a page of the Book, a page of the Book.

separate

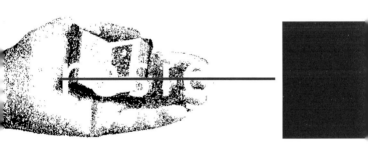

close

river

[   ]

Dread of One Single End

Still to be where we are nothing but this "still" to be lived.

The words of friendship always come before friendship, as if the latter must wait to be announced before it can show itself.

I

We cannot have an image of ourselves.
Do we have one of others?
No doubt, but we never know, alas, if it is the right one.

To see, the way we might say, "see you later," to a stranger we watch leaving.
What passes sheds light on passage.
What remains, annuls it.

Open my name.
Open the book.

The happiness we feel in loving is not necessarily tied to a happy love.
It is a need for love.

In my bathroom mirror I saw a face appear that could have been mine, but whose features I seemed to discover for the first time.

Face of another and yet so familiar.

Sorting through my memories I recognized him as the man I'm mistaken for. I am the only one to know he has always been a stranger to me.

Suddenly the face disappeared, and the mirror, having lost its object, reflected nothing but the bare wall opposite, white and smooth.

Page of glass and page of stone in dialogue, solitary and solidary.

The book has no point of origin.

Young, the world, in the eyes of eternity, and so old in the eyes of the instant.

Do we ask an island who are you?
Flattered and dazzled by the sea.
One day, to be swallowed up.

Fastened to nothing. Fastened to water.

"How do you see freedom?" the disciple asked his teacher.

"Perhaps as two daredevil wings in the sky, fighting desperately against the wind," replied the teacher.

And added: "Remains to be seen, however, if – as you too have supposed – these wings belong to a frail bird of passage."

"And if they were not the wings of a frail bird?" continued the disciple.

"The more fitting," said the teacher then, "the comparison."

"The image of freedom would be the wind."

Each truth works for its truth.
Modest contribution to universal Truth.
Our belief sustains it.

…all these little truths that come to undermine the idea we might have of one unique truth.

– Ants, that's what they are – I thought – imperturbable, digging their holes.

Do not try to use a cam where you need a bolt.

"The Truth does not exist, no doubt to allow our truths to exist," he said.

And added: "Once the sun has set, in the celestial void, we lift our eyes to where millions of stars glitter.

"O solitude of every one of them."

By the light of our insistent truths we wander into death.

Immutable and just, the law. Justice is less sure of itself.

Impossible to grasp, perhaps, the Truth.
Trying to express it we are often led astray.
Disloyal in spite of itself, the first word.

Truth as choice rather than voice?
I believe. I map a course.
Light. Light.

"Truth is an unpronounceable word," he said.

Do not hamper the free flight of an idea. You would be the first to regret your thoughtless gesture.

The soul has no restraints.

The sparrow pays no attention to dogs, but does beware the cat.

Eyes riveted to the clock, trembling with expectation. Every movement of the hand makes you jump because it calls you into question.

So capricious, the future. It always takes us by surprise.

Expecting what, if not death? And yet we dread it. Expecting, perhaps, to be forgotten by death.

God is not in the answer. As the diamond in its reflections, He is in the flash of a question.

Every heart beat is death's punctual answer to the fearful question of the heart and life's evasive answer to the enigmatic question of death.

The body is without projects, without future; those are dreams and desires of the instant that gives it form.

Construct what's running down. Instruct what's being built up.

If I was not here yesterday, why worry if I'll be here tomorrow?

And today, how demonstrate my presence among you if I am unable to furnish proof?

He said: "Do not trust ideas that have traveled more than one road. You won't know which one to take in order to find them.

"Ideas do not come to us. We go toward them the way we return to a spring that has quenched our thirst."

The world is small, so small that the world makes short work of it.

"To increase by nothings.

"Lightweight. Lightweight," he said.

"What nothings are you talking about?" asked, one day, a disciple.

And the sage replied: "The mind sets its goal ever farther. O vertiginous push upward; but what is up unless a perpetual denial of down?"

And he added: "Down here was nothing and up there is nothing – but *between*, light strains through."

All light resides in thought.

By day you lay foundations. By night you doubt.

Memory invented time to its own glory, without noticing that time was already the memory of eternity.

The mirror reflects only one single image of us, the one it has decided to reveal to us.
Test by subtraction.

We can read only one word at a time.

What swims is as old as water.
What breathes is as old as air.
What dims is as old as time.

How can the body in pain manage to attract our attention, except by exhibiting images of its pain?

But the soul?

A soul in pain has no image of itself to offer.

The soul is what causes pain, but suffers alone.

The rushing water gradually loses even the notion of its overwhelming force, which at first had dazzled it.

Then, its pride fallen, it is nothing but domesticated power, in the service of man.

O unsuspected sadness of long impassive rivers.

Flaws, *crapauds* and *jardinages*: misery of the diamond.

Do not ask the ocean to show you the way.
Rather put the question to the reed that has lost it.

As we measure the flow from a source, so we should gauge our output of words.
Be sparing with them, so as not to run dry.

He said: "A vinegar noise." At first this seemed strange, then by and by I got used to the expression, without however understanding it any better.

"Don't I occasionally say: An oily silence?"

And he added:

"Images often speak only to those who use them."

Soul and body are prey to the same illnesses.

Day is sick of images.
Madness. Madness.
Night, sick of oblivion.

There is no true silence except in the symbol's heart of hearts, unexplored.

Winter has covered my pen with snow.

White page, of ice. So young a word and already sentenced.

Ah, to write only resurrected words. To deal only with words of the highest season.

Luminous.

Not to see. Not to know. To be.

To go all the way, then plunge. Chosen.

"We must never leave the sick to their thoughts," wrote a sage, ironically.

"For them, the illness comes before anything. And that is the opposite of wisdom.

"Did not a sick man recently go mad for thinking he really was sick?

"He suffered, unawares, of a different illness."

We die only one death: the one we did not expect.

One flame is not enough for the glory of fire.

As he got older he noticed that one question became more important to him day by day: *how not to get old*?

But he had the question wrong. What he should have asked is: how to keep all the youthfulness of wisdom?

The void is more daring than the whole.

dread

. . . . 2,

Edmond Jabès died in Paris in 1991 at the age of 78. He settled in France after being expelled from his native Egypt with other Jews during the 1956 Suez Crisis. In 1987, he received France's National Grand Prize for Poetry. Other works available in English include *The Book of Questions* (reissued in two volumes in 1991), *The Book of Resemblances* (three volumes, 1990-92), *The Book of Margins* (1993), *the Little Book of Unsuspected Subversion* (1996), and, translated by Keith Waldrop, *If There Were Anywhere But Desert* (1988).

Rosmarie Waldrop's translations of Jabès received a Harold Morton Landon and a Columbia University Translation Center Award. Her recent books of poetry are *Reluctant Gravities* (1999), *Split Infinites* (1998), and *Another Language: Selected Poems* (1997).

Ed Epping has published three other titles with Granary Books, including *Secreted Contract*, *Abstract Refuse* (out-of-print) and *Mettle*, a collaboration with Kimberly Lyons. He is currently director of the School of Art and Design at the University of Illinois in Chicago.

Desire for a Beginning
Dread of One Single End

Designed by Ed Epping.
The images were created on a Power
Macintosh G3 using Macromedia Free-
hand 8, Adobe Photoshop 5 and Adobe
In-Design 1.5.
The text is set in StoneSans and Stone-
Sans italic.
42 copies are specially bound, with
inserts, and are signed by the translator
and artist.